HAL•LEONARD

JAZZ PLAY ALONG®

Book and CD for B♭, E♭, C and Bass Clef Instruments

volume 71

Arranged and Produced
by Mark Taylor

Cole Porter
CLASSICS

10 FAVORITE TUNES

T0081538

BOOK

CD BOOK

ISBN-13: 978-1-4234-2522-9
ISBN-10: 1-4234-2522-7

HAL•LEONARD®
CORPORATION

7777 W. BLUEMOUND RD. P.O. BOX 13819 MILWAUKEE, WI 53213

Visit Hal Leonard Online at
www.halleonard.com

Cole Porter Classics

Volume 71

Arranged and Produced by
Mark Taylor

Featured Players:

Graham Breedlove–Trumpet
John Desalme–Saxophones
Tony Nalker–Piano
Jim Roberts–Bass
Steve Fidyk–Drums

HOW TO USE THE CD:

Each song has <u>two</u> tracks:

1) Split Track/Melody

Woodwind, Brass, Keyboard, and **Mallet Players** can use this track as a learning tool for melody style and inflection.

Bass Players can learn and perform with this track – remove the recorded bass track by turning down the volume on the LEFT channel.

Keyboard and **Guitar Players** can learn and perform with this track – remove the recorded piano part by turning down the volume on the RIGHT channel.

2) Full Stereo Track

Soloists or **Groups** can learn and perform with this accompaniment track with the RHYTHM SECTION only.

DREAM DANCING

WORDS AND MUSIC BY
COLE PORTER

FROM THIS MOMENT ON

WORDS AND MUSIC BY
COLE PORTER

C VERSION

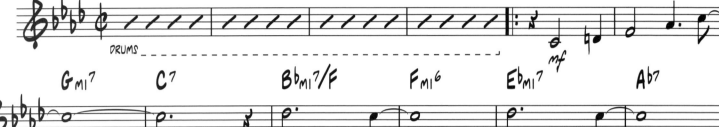

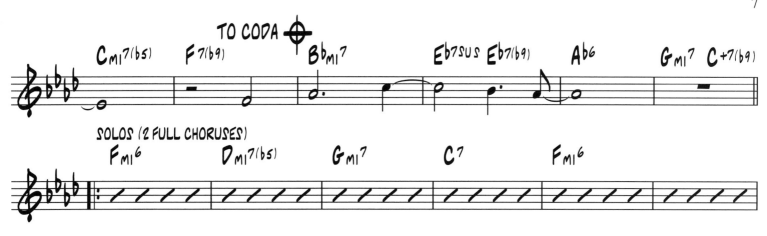

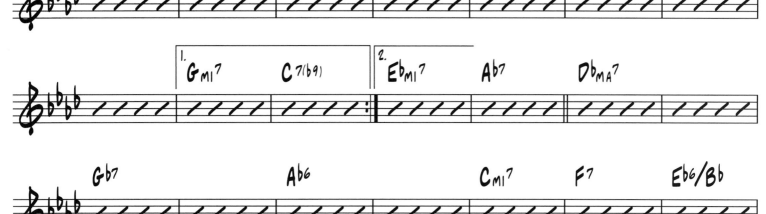

I GET A KICK OUT OF YOU

WORDS AND MUSIC BY
COLE PORTER

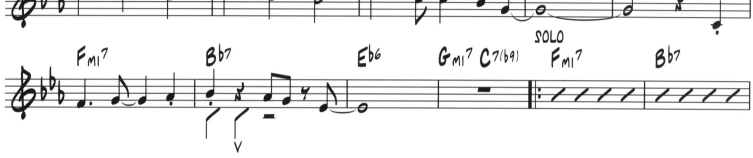

I LOVE PARIS

FROM CAN-CAN
FROM HIGH SOCIETY

WORDS AND MUSIC
BY COLE PORTER

C VERSION

JUST ONE OF THOSE THINGS

WORDS AND MUSIC BY
COLE PORTER

LOVE FOR SALE

WORDS AND MUSIC BY
COLE PORTER

CD
13 : SPLIT TRACK/MELODY
14 : FULL STEREO TRACK

C VERSION MEDIUM LATIN

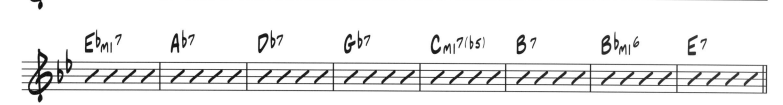

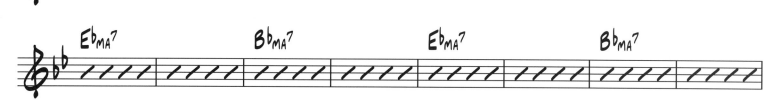

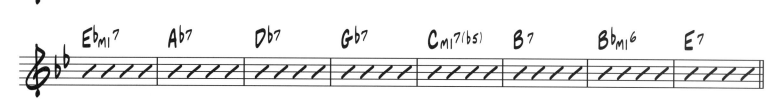

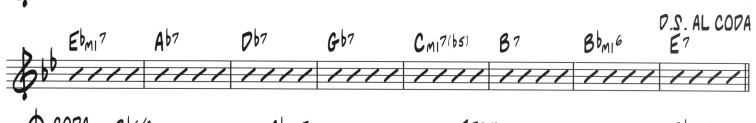

MY HEART BELONGS TO DADDY

CD
15 : SPLIT TRACK/MELODY
16 : FULL STEREO TRACK

C VERSION

WORDS AND MUSIC BY
COLE PORTER

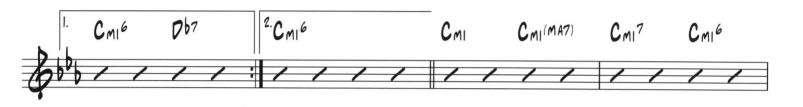

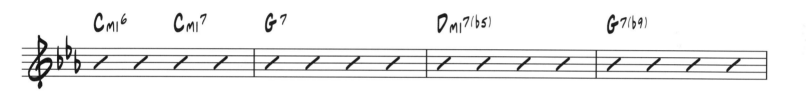

NIGHT AND DAY

WORDS AND MUSIC BY
COLE PORTER

C VERSION

MEDIUM SWING

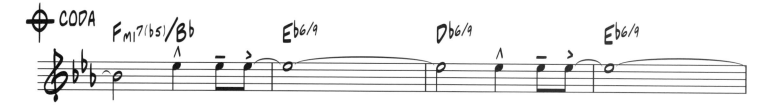

WHAT IS THIS THING CALLED LOVE?

CD
19 : SPLIT TRACK/MELODY
20 : FULL STEREO TRACK

C VERSION

WORDS AND MUSIC BY
COLE PORTER

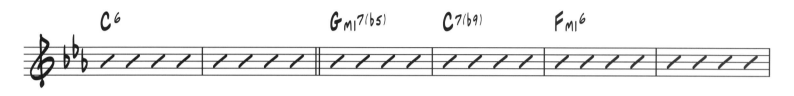

I'VE GOT MY EYES ON YOU

CD
◆9 : SPLIT TRACK/MELODY
◆10 : FULL STEREO TRACK

C VERSION

WORDS AND MUSIC BY
COLE PORTER

I'VE GOT MY EYES ON YOU

WORDS AND MUSIC BY
COLE PORTER

CD
- ♦ 9 : SPLIT TRACK/MELODY
- 10 : FULL STEREO TRACK

Dream Dancing

Words and Music by
Cole Porter

CD

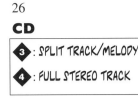

FROM THIS MOMENT ON

WORDS AND MUSIC BY
COLE PORTER

Bb VERSION

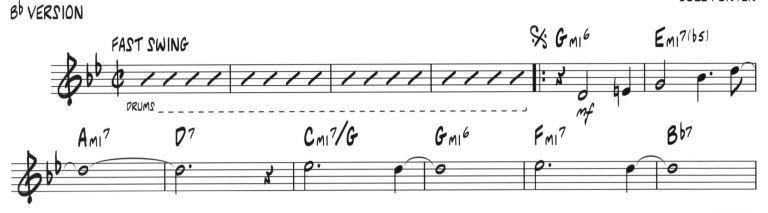

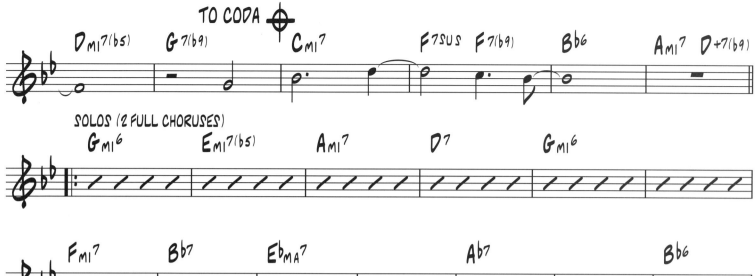

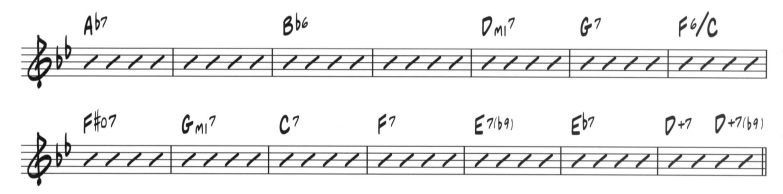

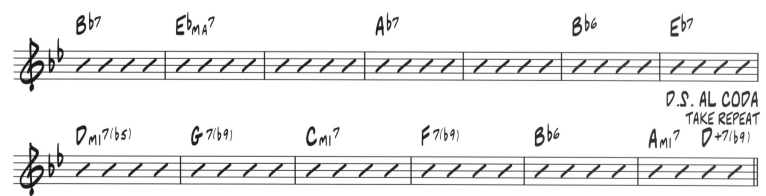

I GET A KICK OUT OF YOU

WORDS AND MUSIC BY
COLE PORTER

Bb VERSION   2 FEEL

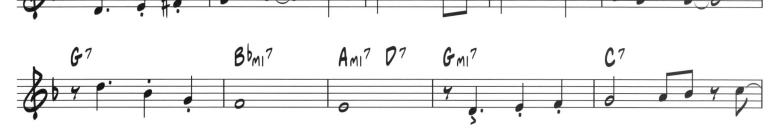

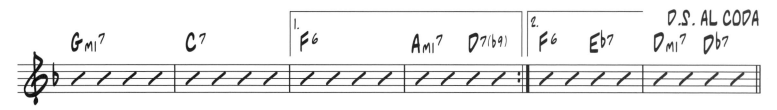

I LOVE PARIS

FROM CAN-CAN
FROM HIGH SOCIETY

WORDS AND MUSIC
BY COLE PORTER

Bb VERSION

SOFT SAMBA

LOVE FOR SALE

WORDS AND MUSIC BY
COLE PORTER

CD
13: SPLIT TRACK/MELODY
14: FULL STEREO TRACK

B♭ VERSION

CD

15 : SPLIT TRACK/MELODY
16 : FULL STEREO TRACK

MY HEART BELONGS TO DADDY

WORDS AND MUSIC BY
COLE PORTER

B♭ VERSION

SOFT LATIN

TO CODA

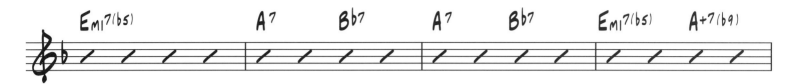

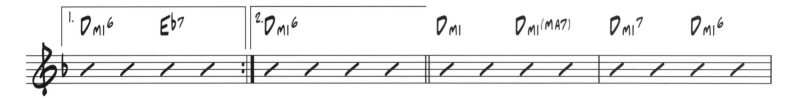

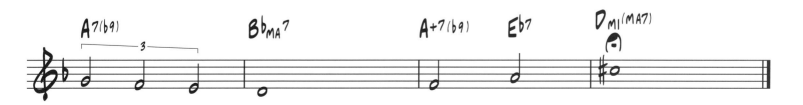

NIGHT AND DAY

WORDS AND MUSIC BY
COLE PORTER

Bb VERSION

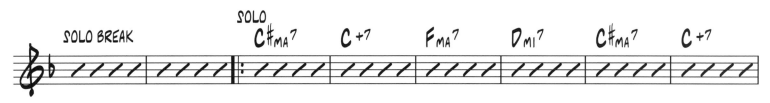

CD
19 : SPLIT TRACK/MELODY
20 : FULL STEREO TRACK

WHAT IS THIS THING CALLED LOVE?

WORDS AND MUSIC BY
COLE PORTER

Bb VERSION

FAST SWING

DRUMS

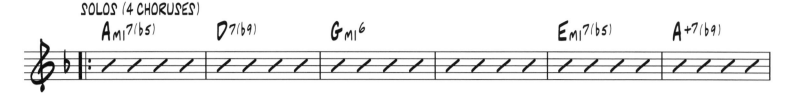

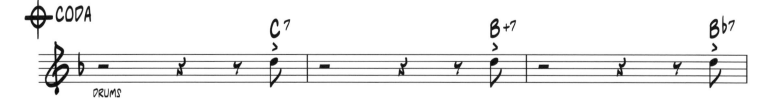

DREAM DANCING

WORDS AND MUSIC BY
COLE PORTER

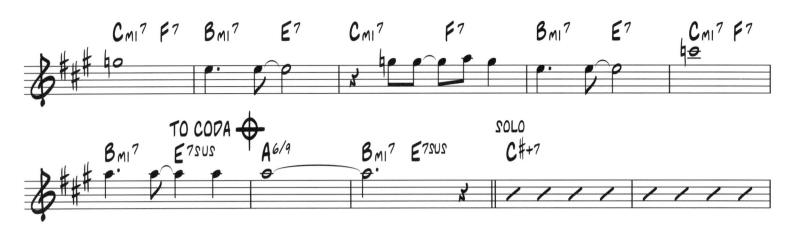

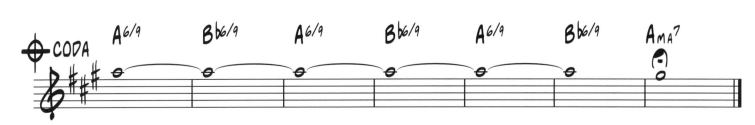

FROM THIS MOMENT ON

WORDS AND MUSIC BY
COLE PORTER

Eb VERSION

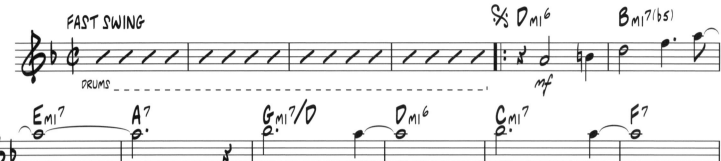

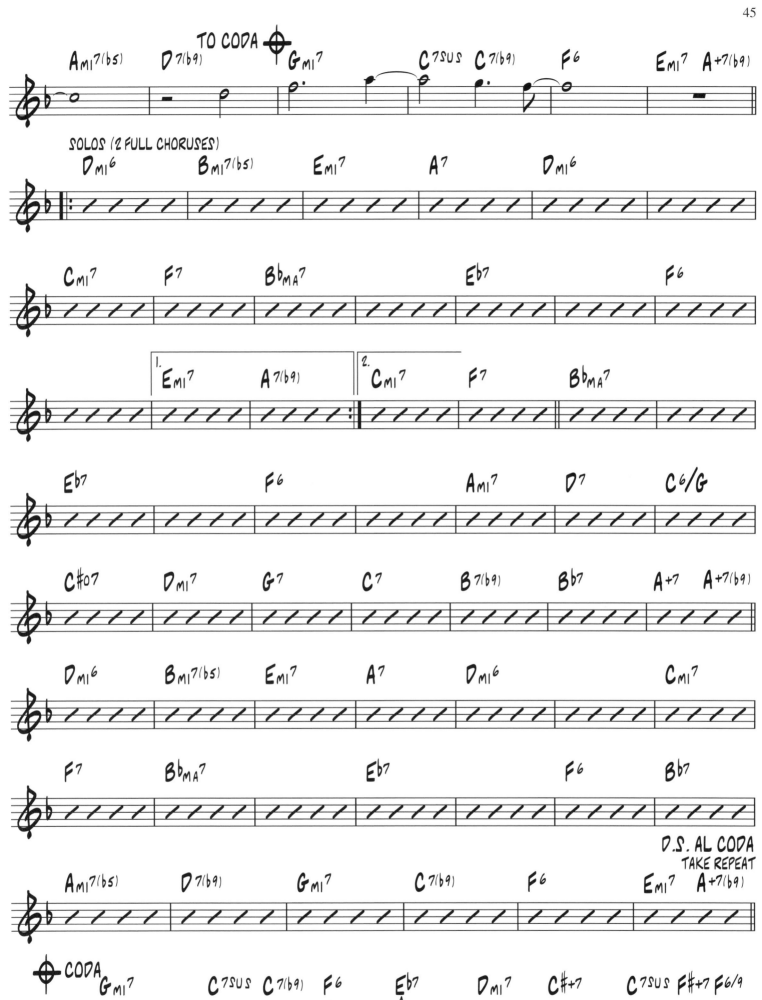

I GET A KICK OUT OF YOU

WORDS AND MUSIC BY
COLE PORTER

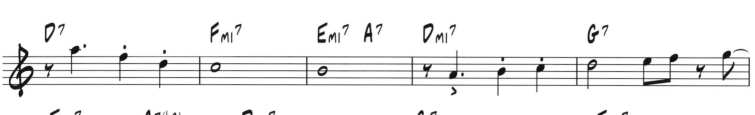

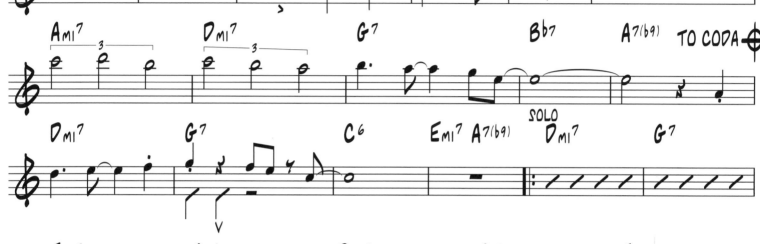

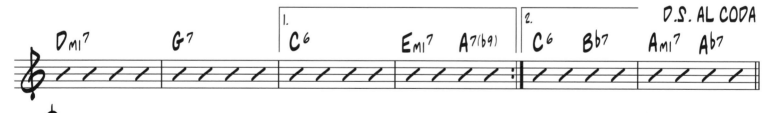

I LOVE PARIS

FROM CAN-CAN
FROM HIGH SOCIETY

WORDS AND MUSIC
BY COLE PORTER

E♭ VERSION

JUST ONE OF THOSE THINGS

WORDS AND MUSIC BY
COLE PORTER

LOVE FOR SALE

WORDS AND MUSIC BY
COLE PORTER

MY HEART BELONGS TO DADDY

CD
15: SPLIT TRACK/MELODY
16: FULL STEREO TRACK

WORDS AND MUSIC BY
COLE PORTER

E♭ VERSION

SOFT LATIN

NIGHT AND DAY

WORDS AND MUSIC BY
COLE PORTER

CD
17 : SPLIT TRACK/MELODY
18 : FULL STEREO TRACK

E♭ VERSION

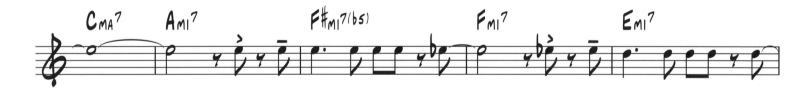

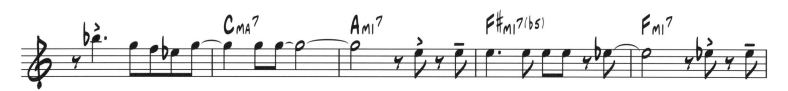

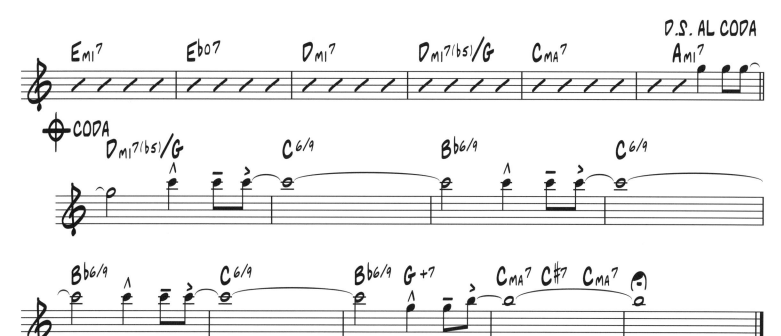

WHAT IS THIS THING CALLED LOVE?

CD

19 : SPLIT TRACK/MELODY
20 : FULL STEREO TRACK

Eb VERSION

WORDS AND MUSIC BY
COLE PORTER

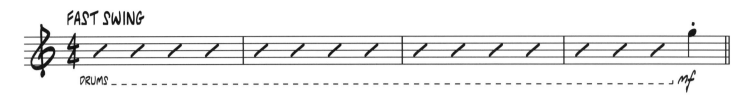

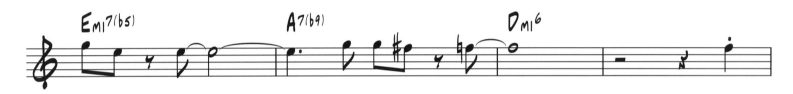

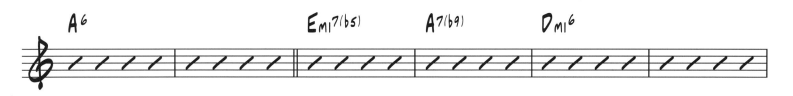

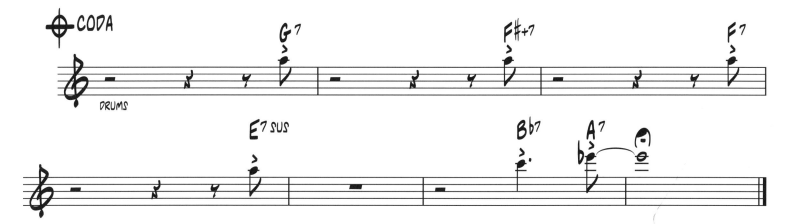

I'VE GOT MY EYES ON YOU

WORDS AND MUSIC BY
COLE PORTER

I'VE GOT MY EYES ON YOU

WORDS AND MUSIC BY
COLE PORTER

Dream Dancing

WORDS AND MUSIC BY
COLE PORTER

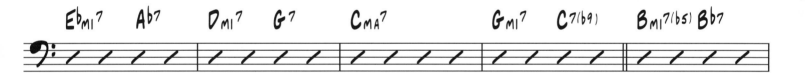

FROM THIS MOMENT ON

WORDS AND MUSIC BY
COLE PORTER

𝄢: C VERSION

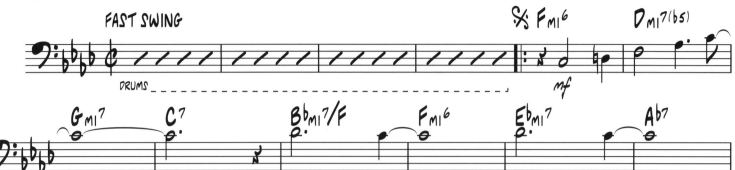

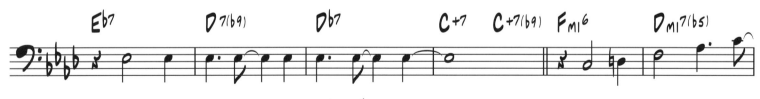

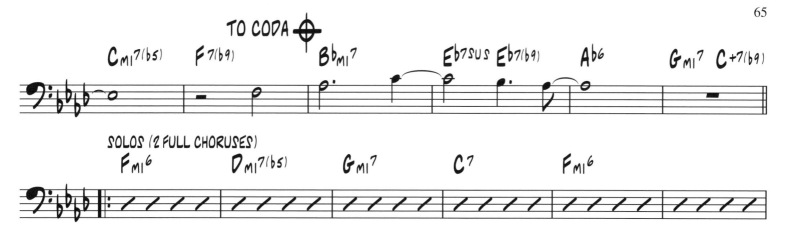

I GET A KICK OUT OF YOU

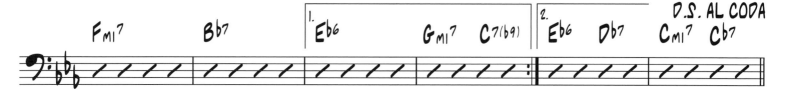

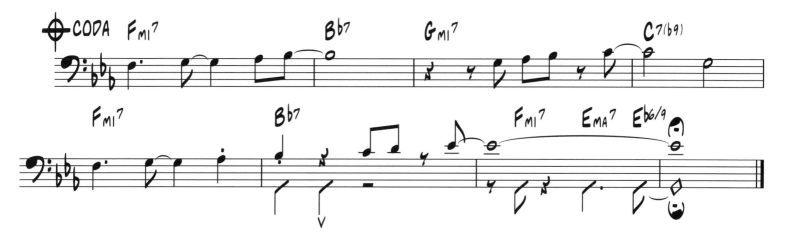

CD

I LOVE PARIS
FROM CAN-CAN
FROM HIGH SOCIETY

WORDS AND MUSIC
BY COLE PORTER

: C VERSION

SOFT SAMBA

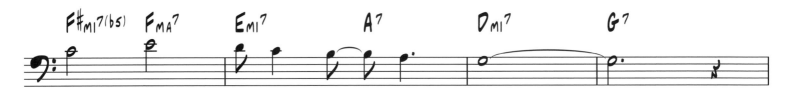

LOVE FOR SALE

CD
13 : SPLIT TRACK/MELODY
14 : FULL STEREO TRACK

WORDS AND MUSIC BY
COLE PORTER

𝄢: C VERSION

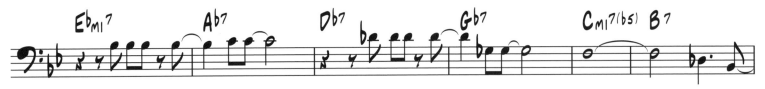

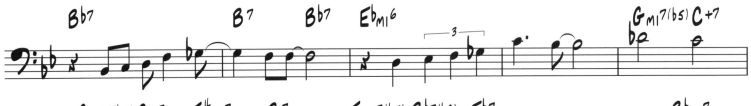

MY HEART BELONGS TO DADDY

WORDS AND MUSIC BY
COLE PORTER

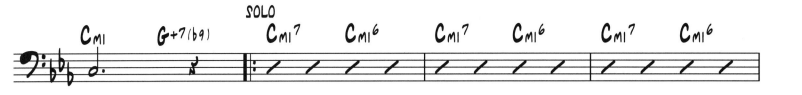

NIGHT AND DAY

WORDS AND MUSIC BY
COLE PORTER

C VERSION   MEDIUM SWING

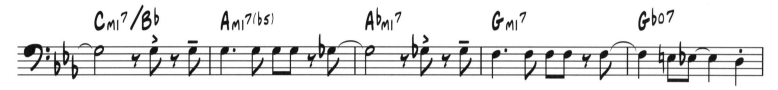

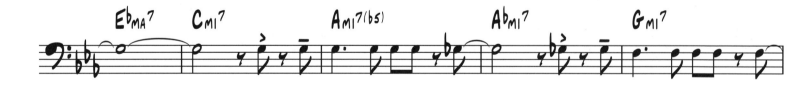

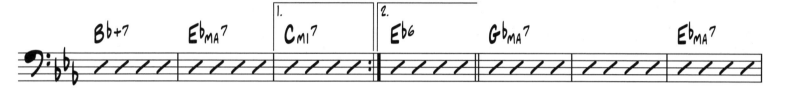

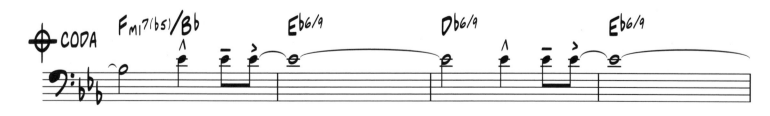

WHAT IS THIS THING CALLED LOVE?

WORDS AND MUSIC BY
COLE PORTER

𝄢: C VERSION

FAST SWING

DRUMS _____ mf

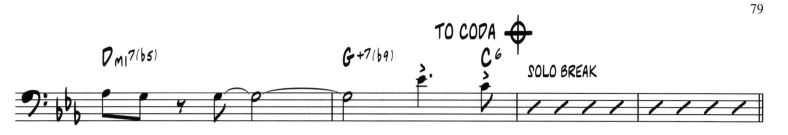

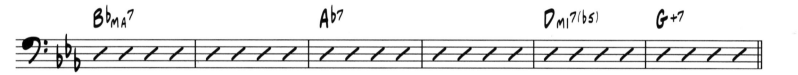

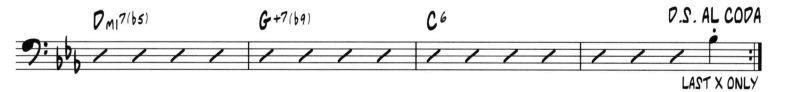

 **Presenting the Hal Leonard JAZZ PLAY ALONG SERIES**

DUKE ELLINGTON Vol. 1 00841644 .... $15.95	**WAYNE SHORTER Vol. 22** 00843015 .... $14.95	**GERRY MULLIGAN CLASSICS Vol. 43** 00843039 .... $16.95	**A CHARLIE BROWN CHRISTMAS Vol. 66** 00843067 .... $14.95
MILES DAVIS Vol. 2 00841645 .... $15.95	**LATIN JAZZ Vol. 23** 00843016 .... $16.95	**OLIVER NELSON Vol. 44** 00843040 .... $15.95	**CHICK COREA Vol. 67** 00843068 .... $14.95
THE BLUES Vol. 3 00841646 .... $15.95	**EARLY JAZZ STANDARDS Vol. 24** 00843017 .... $14.95	**JAZZ AT THE MOVIES Vol. 45** 00843041 .... $14.95	**CHARLES MINGUS Vol. 68** 00843069 .... $16.95
JAZZ BALLADS Vol. 4 00841691 .... $15.95	**CHRISTMAS JAZZ Vol. 25** 00843018 .... $15.95	**BROADWAY JAZZ STANDARDS Vol. 46** 00843042 .... $14.95	**CLASSIC JAZZ Vol. 69** 00843071 .... $14.95
BEST OF BEBOP Vol. 5 00841689 .... $15.95	**CHARLIE PARKER Vol. 26** 00843019 .... $16.95	**CLASSIC JAZZ BALLADS Vol. 47** 00843043 .... $14.95	**THE DOORS Vol. 70** 00843072 .... $14.95
JAZZ CLASSICS WITH EASY CHANGES Vol. 6 00841690 .... $15.95	**GREAT JAZZ STANDARDS Vol. 27** 00843020 .... $14.95	**BEBOP CLASSICS Vol. 48** 00843044 .... $14.95	**COLE PORTER CLASSICS Vol. 71** 00843073 .... $14.95
ESSENTIAL JAZZ STANDARDS Vol. 7 00843000 .... $15.95	**BIG BAND ERA Vol. 28** 00843021 .... $14.95	**MILES DAVIS STANDARDS Vol. 49** 00843045 .... $16.95	**CLASSIC JAZZ BALLADS Vol. 72** 00843074 .... $14.95
ANTONIO CARLOS JOBIM AND THE ART OF THE BOSSA NOVA Vol. 8 00843001 .... $15.95	**LENNON AND McCARTNEY Vol. 29** 00843022 .... $16.95	**GREAT JAZZ CLASSICS Vol. 50** 00843046 .... $14.95	**JAZZ/BLUES Vol. 73** 00843075 .... $14.95
DIZZY GILLESPIE Vol. 9 00843002 .... $15.95	**BLUES' BEST Vol. 30** 00843023 .... $14.95	**UP-TEMPO JAZZ Vol. 51** 00843047 .... $14.95	

DIZZY GILLESPIE Vol. 9 00843002 .... $15.95	**JAZZ IN THREE Vol. 31** 00843024 .... $14.95	**STEVIE WONDER Vol. 52** 00843048 .... $14.95
DISNEY CLASSICS Vol. 10 00843003 .... $15.95	**BEST OF SWING Vol. 32** 00843025 .... $14.95	**RHYTHM CHANGES Vol. 53** 00843049 .... $14.95
RODGERS AND HART FAVORITES Vol. 11 00843004 .... $15.95	**SONNY ROLLINS Vol. 33** 00843029 .... $14.95	**"MOONLIGHT IN VERMONT" AND OTHER GREAT STANDARDS Vol. 54** 00843050 .... $14.95
ESSENTIAL JAZZ CLASSICS Vol. 12 00843005 .... $15.95	**ALL TIME STANDARDS Vol. 34** 00843030 .... $14.95	**BENNY GOLSON Vol. 55** 00843052 .... $14.95
JOHN COLTRANE Vol. 13 00843006 .... $15.95	**BLUESY JAZZ Vol. 35** 00843031 .... $14.95	**VINCE GUARALDI Vol. 57** 00843057 .... $14.95
IRVING BERLIN Vol. 14 00843007 .... $14.95	**HORACE SILVER Vol. 36** 00843032 .... $14.95	**MORE LENNON AND McCARTNEY Vol. 58** 00843059 .... $14.95
RODGERS & HAMMERSTEIN Vol. 15 00843008 .... $14.95	**BILL EVANS Vol. 37** 00843033 .... $16.95	**SOUL JAZZ Vol. 59** 00843060 .... $14.95
COLE PORTER Vol. 16 00843009 .... $15.95	**YULETIDE JAZZ Vol. 38** 00843034 .... $14.95	**MONGO SANTAMARIA Vol. 61** 00843062 .... $14.95
COUNT BASIE Vol. 17 00843010 .... $15.95	**"ALL THE THINGS YOU ARE" & MORE JEROME KERN SONGS Vol. 39** 00843035 .... $14.95	**JAZZ-ROCK FUSION Vol. 62** 00843063 .... $14.95
HAROLD ARLEN Vol. 18 00843011 .... $14.95	**BOSSA NOVA Vol. 40** 00843036 .... $14.95	**CLASSICAL JAZZ Vol. 63** 00843064 .... $14.95
COOL JAZZ Vol. 19 00843012 .... $15.95	**CLASSIC DUKE ELLINGTON Vol. 41** 00843037 .... $14.95	**TV TUNES Vol. 64** 00843065 .... $14.95
CHRISTMAS CAROLS Vol. 20 00843080 .... $14.95	**GERRY MULLIGAN FAVORITES Vol. 42** 00843038 .... $16.95	**SMOOTH JAZZ Vol. 65** 00843066 .... $14.95
RODGERS AND HART CLASSICS Vol. 21 00843014 .... $14.95		

FOR MORE INFORMATION,
SEE YOUR LOCAL MUSIC DEALER,
OR WRITE TO:

HAL•LEONARD®
CORPORATION
7777 W. BLUEMOUND RD. P.O. BOX 13819
MILWAUKEE, WISCONSIN 53213

Visit Hal Leonard online at
www.halleonard.com

0507